This Is a Let's-Read-and-Find-Out Science Book®

My Feet
by Aliki

Thomas Y. Crowell   New York

For all my friends at

Miller, Mission Avenue, Scottish Corners, Anderson, Indianola,

Olde Orchard, Douglas, Worthington Estates, Brookside, Colonial Hills,

London, Havens, Hillcrest, Woodlawn, and all the rest—

with love

♥

The *Let's-Read-and-Find-Out Science Book* series was originated by Dr. Franklyn M. Branley, Astronomer Emeritus and former Chairman of the American Museum–Hayden Planetarium, and was formerly co-edited by him and Dr. Roma Gans, Professor Emeritus of Childhood Education, Teachers College, Columbia University. For a complete catalog of Let's-Read-and-Find-Out Science Books, write to Thomas Y. Crowell Junior Books, Harper & Row, Publishers, Inc., 10 East 53rd Street, New York, NY 10022.

Let's-Read-and-Find-Out Science Book is a registered trademark of Harper & Row, Publishers, Inc.

Library of Congress Cataloging-in-Publication Data
Aliki.
   My feet / by Aliki.
      p.   cm. — (Let's-read-and-find-out science book)
      Summary: Brief text and illustrations describe the various parts
of the foot and all the things feet help us to do.
      ISBN 0-690-04813-0 : $. — ISBN 0-690-04815-7 (lib. bdg.) :
$
      1. Foot—Juvenile literature. [1. Foot.] I. Title.
II. Series.
QM549.A45   1990   89-49357
612'.98—dc20   CIP
                                                            AC

My Feet

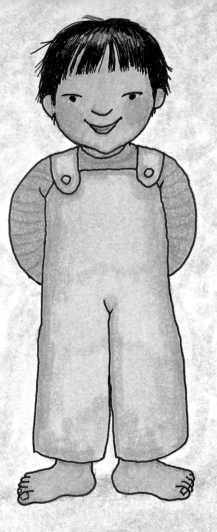

I have two feet.
My feet are the part of my body I stand on.

Each foot has a front—the toes.

It has a back—the heel.

And it has an underneath   the sole.

toes

sole

heel

5

I have ten toes I can wiggle—
five on my left foot, five on my right foot.
There is a big toe, a little toe, and three toes in between.

Each toe has a nail to protect it.
Toenails grow fast.
It tickles when my mother cuts mine.

The heel bone is big.

It is strong.

It helps support my weight.

Sometimes for fun, I walk on my heels.
It's even harder to stand still on them.
Try it!

I can feel another strong bone on the sole of my foot.

It is padded with a soft cushion of skin.

That is the ball of the foot.

When I jump, I jump on the balls of my feet.

There is a curved arch under each foot, too,
right in the middle of the sole.
When I make footprints, my arch doesn't print.

But some people have flat feet.
Their arches aren't very curved.

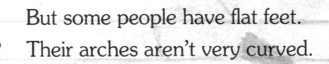

Feet come in all sizes.

They grow as we grow.

My feet grow so fast, I have to get them measured whenever I buy new shoes.

12

My sister has tiny feet.
They fit into the palm of my hand.

My brother's feet are bigger than mine.

My mother's feet are bigger than his.
(Sometimes she wears high heels.
She says they are not very comfortable.)

My father's feet are the biggest of all!

Whatever size they are, we use our feet all the time.
They take us where we want to go.
I keep mine busy.

I walk,   I run,

I skip,   I march,   I kick.

I hop,

I tiptoe,

18

I skate,

I dance.

When I do these things,
I try to think of what part
of my foot I am using.
My toes? My heel?
Or all of my foot?
It's a game you can play, too.

I am lucky I have two feet that work well.

My friend doesn't.

There are many things she can't do.

But with her crutches she can walk as fast as I can.

I have fun with my feet.
I play with them.
I can clap my feet and rub them together.

BRAVO!

I can pick things up with my toes.
I can even draw with my toes—but not well!

I dress my feet.
I put on my socks first.

I wear sneakers for play,

and fancy shoes when I dress up.

I wear galoshes when it rains,

or sandals when it's hot.

I like bare feet best!
But I have to be careful.

In winter I put on heavy socks and boots.

I play in the snow until my feet are freezing cold.

30

Then I run home and soak them, and put on my slippers.
When my feet are warm, the rest of me is too.

Right now, I feel cozy from head to toe.
I'll give my feet a rest and read a book.